MY BELOVED

CORTNIE FITZSIMMONS

ISBN 979-8-88685-831-0 (paperback)
ISBN 979-8-88685-832-7 (digital)

Christian Faith Publishing
832 Park Avenue
Meadville, PA 16335
www.christianfaithpublishing.com

All scriptures quoted came from Nelson, Thomas. Holy Bible, NKJV, Thomas Nelson Publishing, 1982.

Printed in the United States of America

CONTENTS

Preface

I'd like to share something simple to understand yet so beautifully profound about our Father in heaven:

If you have children, you know that our natural inclination is to love, nurture, and protect them; all natural emotions are given by God, and we know Jesus's sacrifice, but the Father denied Himself of this right and gave His Son for us.

"For God so loved the world that He gave His only begotten Son, that whoever believes in Him should not perish but have everlasting life" (John 3:16 NKJV).

The embodiment, the very epitome of love, became flesh and dwelt among us. The very essence of the Father's love was manifested through His Son, Jesus. When I think of the agonizing pain the Father must've felt leading His own Son to the slaughter, who would do this? But God!

Even though humanity rejected Him, He said, "I choose you, I choose love, I choose to give my heart my precious son, so we can be one again"

I think of the hunger that the Father had to be reunited with His creation, crying out to us deep unto deep.

Jesus came willingly: *"No one takes it from Me, but I lay it down Myself. I have power to lay it down, and I have power to take it again. This commandment I have received from My Father"* (John 10:18 NKJV).

With His life, He became the bridge so we could cross the path and be united with the Father, a love that said, "Break me, whip me, kill me, so that you can be free." It's a love of reckless abandonment of self to save our souls. The perfect sacrifice where blood and water flowed, a love where light and darkness clashed, and light overcame it. Who does this? But God!

The Spirit that made heaven and earth raised Jesus and many others from the dead, given to us to dwell in our inner being, the very breath (Ruach) of Godhead in our imperfect vessels, given by a perfect God. He made a way where there was none.

He came, He walked among us, and He conquered. Who does this? But God!

Our Father loves deep, He loves hard, and He chose to do whatever it takes to be reunited with His children.

"For in Him we live we move and have our being, as also some of your own poets have said, 'For we are also His offspring'" (Acts 17:28 NKJV).

We are deeply loved; this is his heart for us!

His Beauty Met My Pain

The Lord Jesus Christ is my saving grace. My favorite scripture is, *"He sent from above, He took me; He drew me out of many waters"* (Psalm 18:16 NKJV). He is my beloved Yeshua Hamashiach, the most beautiful name above all names. I pray that my adoration and thoughts of Him become your own and that it ignites a longing and a desire in you to grow closer to Him, to sit at His feet, and drink from the cup that never runs dry.

Yeshua Hamashiach
Without His guiding hand, this book would not be in existence.

You Love Me

*In him we were also chosen, having been predestined according to
the plan of him who works out everything in conformity with the purpose of his will.*

—Ephesians 1:11 (NIV)

I will place my failures and my sin out in the wide open for the whole world to see
that your grace is sufficient for me.
If it speaks to a heart or a soul,
your glory they need to know.
In a world that snares and judges me for the things I've done,
you love me, and we are one.
I will pour out my heart to them; they need to know of your peace and your forgiveness.
I will show them my heartache and my pain,
the many tears I've shed pouring out like rain.
Lord, let this give them hope,
that you bring the drowning afloat.

Chapter I

Testimony

KNOCKING

I the Lord, have called You in righteousness, And will hold Your hand; I will keep You and give You as a covenant to the people, As a light to the Gentiles, To open blind eyes, to bring out prisoners from the prison, Those who sit in darkness from the prison house.

—Isaiah 42:6–7 (NKJV)

He stands there patiently knocking at the door,
Believe it, He's alive forevermore,
He will bless you with His glorious love, then you will be seeing
A river of His love flowing through your being,
Is it so hard to believe?
He is alive, the holy one, are we fit to lay at His feet?
Stop fighting what is in your heart you know is true.
Let His holiness heal you, He is the only one who can set you free.
I tell you He is alive, let Him hear your plea.
How much more of this emptiness can you take?
He stands there, patiently knocking, what choice will you make?

I Welcome You, Lord

Your sweet embrace,
Your love that will never change,
That moment of sweet surrender.
In your presence is where I want to live forever,
The moment where my brokenness meets your grace,
I can feel your love throughout my entire being,
I just linger—receiving.
Just a little taste of your glory,
Oh, my king, most high, hold me.
Let me lose myself completely in your sweet embrace,
Where nothing else matters but that I am in you,
You are all I see in this place. Where I am free,
Oh, Lord, you amaze me!

BOUND

Then Jesus spoke to them again, saying, "I am the light of the world. He who follows me shall not walk in darkness but have the light of life."

—John 8:12 (NKJV)

I would look at you and smile, telling myself it'll be okay, the pills won't wear off for a while.
No one knew what I was on, slowly losing myself to this drug.
I acted like I was okay, but inside, I was crying out for love.
Screaming inside for someone to rescue me, I look happy, but I'm a good actor.
Open your eyes and see. I try to cover up the bleeding wounds, only creating more scars.
I'm looking at you now, but my thoughts run afar.
I should be happy, I have a wonderful husband and a beautiful child, but I'm not.
I hide it so well, my husband's eyes pleading with me to STOP.
He doesn't know how to reach me; he feels hopeless and lost.
Two years, I was addicted, and I'm thankful still to this day my son doesn't know.
I was consumed with depression, anxiety, and fear.
I had hit rock bottom; I wasn't thinking clear,
someone did see, someone did care.
He healed my wounds with His love, and it overshadowed the terror.
He gave me peace and strength to live my life as I should.
JESUS is the one who saved me. The only name that could.

Breaking Point

He sent from above, He took me, He drew me out of many waters.

—2 Samuel 22:17 (NKJV)

I sat there; sad, weary, and very much alone. My heart and
soul felt like they were dying, unbearable
darkness I have known; it sucked me into a web of hurt and self-denial.
The pain simmered inside me while I asked myself over
and over why my life was so worthwhile.
I sat there, and I wept inside. I wouldn't leave my home, so there I would hide.
I couldn't take it. I just wanted to die.
Then I went to the house of God and felt His love surrounding
Me, I could no longer walk away from Him, the beauty of what my soul had seen.
My soul cried out for my savior, myself so emotionally beaten, my mind so unclean,
"Oh, take me, Lord," I asked.
My soul so battered and dry, then nothing but peace as the
Lord Almighty breathed life into my weary soul.
I shook, and I cried, for my Messiah had made me whole.
I knew then I could never turn my back on Him, for I need
Him like I need air, in a world so lonely and unfair—
all I did was ask, and He healed me with His loving care.

MY SISTERS

There is a way that seems right to a man, But its end is the way of death

—Proverbs 16:25 (NKJV)

You drift from one day to the next, miserable and stubborn you are.
You live in fear of your own shadow, you're so broken and fragile.
Your soul wanders in darkness, and you wonder why you grieve.
Your emptiness has overtaken you, now you are so low you long to be numb.
Your heart beats, but you are not alive.
You've lost all the love and hope that was once in your life.
You float throughout the day and long for it to be over.
You deny all things that are true and are blind to them.
Oh, how I wish you would open your eyes to all the lies you have believed.
Lies that have become who you are.
Do you even know who you are anymore?
When this was me, I didn't.
The darkness overcame me, and I lived in it, begging it to go away.
Yet also feeling it was all I knew.
It doesn't go away; it continues to haunt you, to suck the life out of you.
Until there is no more life left.
Then it stays making sure you stay deprived.
You can act like you're happy, but I can see right through you.
You are beaten down, bruised, and mangled.
Stop acting like you're too proud or letting stubbornness keep you.
I can see you weeping inside.
How much can you take of this cruel world that is not your friend?
I tell you; you will not find comfort in this place.
So what are you going to do about it? Watch yourself disintegrate?
Or make the choice you've known deep down all along.

Torn

*Wives, likewise, be submissive to your own husbands, that if even some do not obey
the word, they, without a word, may be won by the conduct of their wives.*

—1 Peter 3:1 (NKJV)

My heart is aching within me; my heart feels like it's been torn into two.
I love you, Lord Jesus; you turned my black sky shiny blue.
You rescued me from death and gave me life when I had none.
The man I chose to spend my life with doesn't know God's first Son.
There is a dark place in my husband, where pain turned into unbelief; now he doesn't believe in my loved one.
He holds the memory against you, Lord, a deep wound.
The greatest love and happiness I have ever known, and I cannot share it with the one who holds my heart.
The day I came to you, I knew; this love I couldn't share with him. A wedge put in our closeness
Pulling us apart.
It's like I'm living a separate life that my husband has no part of.
He doesn't object to me living for you, but he hasn't come to know my true love.
Lord, break the chains that are keeping him from you.
I long for him to know and believe your truth.

What Will You Teach Your Children?

I wasn't raised in a rich family; I grew up watching my mom struggle to get by
The days were hard for her; I used to watch her cry.
I remember being dropped off at daycare, the sun barely rising in the sky.
She would get off work, and it would already be dark outside.
I would look at her; see the exhaustion on her face, her tired eyes.
She didn't have time to volunteer at my school like the other moms did,
I didn't get kissed or hugged much; she didn't receive that either when she was a kid.
What she did give me was more important than all the above; she taught me about the messiah.
I can remember being at church on Sunday evenings when my sisters and I started messing around
She would pinch our legs.
I remember her worshipping the Lord with her arms outstretched and tears falling down her face.
When all seemed so overwhelming in her life the joy, she had because of Him.
She would dress us in our fluffy dresses, matching purses, and shiny shoes; she was happy he was her will to live.
I can recall the happiness I saw in and through her: I was in awe of this Jesus.
Now I know how she feels; His love carries us.
So what could I say of my mom?
Now we can sing to our Savior a new love song.

THE SEED

I have planted, Apollos watered; but God gave the increase.

—1 Corinthians 3:6

I had a dream; I saw my father in heaven in all His glory and grace.
Words cannot describe Him, His overpowering love filled the heavens, oh, His face!
I never wanted to look away from Him; He told me to turn my head, and look, He talked.
through His eyes,
I turned my head and saw this heavenly being, all I could do was sigh.
She didn't compare to Him, but oh, how lovely she is; He told me it was her in her heavenly
form; she had unwavering faith. Now her soul shows;
she radiated with heavenly peace.
He instructed me to go to her and tell her what my heart knows.
I floated to her presence and told her it was because of her faith that led me back to Him, and
now I am in heaven.
Tears of joy illuminated from her essence,
I told her, "All the times you told me I needed Christ, I didn't listen,
but I heard, and it followed me. His name was planted firm, also what I was raised to
believe. So I thank you for not giving up on my weary soul;
you'll never know how those words took hold."
We walked to our Lord whom we hold in the highest favor.
I took her by the hand and said, "Mom, let's go worship our SAVIOR."

Please Listen

Keep your heart with all diligence, for out of it spring the issues of life.

—Proverbs 4:23 (NKJV)

You think that you are in love, so you give him all that you are.
Not knowing the emptiness that will soon follow leaving a scar.
The soul tie that was formed in the spirit from becoming one flesh.
Now you're all broken up, a mess.
You did it, realizing later, you weren't ready.
The relationship didn't last; now you're left alone feeling heavy.
You gave more than you should; you'd take it back if you could.
That's why the Lord says, "Wait until you are married; it ties you to that person in a strong way."
So as the days move on, you feel a piece of you is gone.
This is one of the reasons why there is so much pain in people's lives.
Children grow up lacking because their moms were too young.
Fatherless daughters and sons,
listen to what I say; this is not the way.
Infections and diseases that are harming and killing people every day.
So many with lost hope and crumbled dreams.
If you are doing it now, you can stop; it's not too late.
Ask the Lord to help you to overcome the desire;
break the soul ties; He is a consuming fire.

SMOKING

Do you not know that to whom you present yourselves as slaves to obey, you are the ones slave whom you obey, whether sin leading to death or, or of obedience leading to righteousness.

—Romans 6:16 (NKJV)

I pushed you away, I knew I should hang on.
My flesh was crying out for what I knew was wrong.
My stress was high, my soul was crying out, "No," inside.
I didn't listen. I ran right back into the worldly comfort I used to know well.
I inhaled, knowing I had entered back into the darkness.
It was just as I had remembered it, lonely and cold, my old best friend, alone.
I was ashamed and started the old cycle again, the counterfeit escape.
Turning my back on my true love.
Shine down on me, holy one.
Take me back to you, Lord. My soul is crying out for your touch.
Heal me again, my king, have mercy on me. I need you so much.
I miss you. You're my love song.
Come back to me, Lord, take me back to where I belong.
Forgive me, Lord, I've been doing wrong,
Help me to leave this behind again to find my way back to you.
You are the only one who shines in truth.
I need you to get through the day.
Jesus, light my way.
All throughout beating myself up, clothing myself again with shame and condemnation,
He continually reminds me that never will He leave me, never will He forsake me
That He will hold me, and together, we'll make it through.
To trust in Him and have faith, once I pull through, this'll be just a memory of yesterday.

CHAPTER 2

Worship

My Soul's Desire

My soul longs, yes, even faints for the courts of the LORD; My
heart and my flesh cry out for the living God.

—Psalm 84:2 (NKJV)

Let my passion for you spring anew,
Give me thoughts of love, thoughts of truth,
Thoughts of you burn deep,
Cut through to the very depths of my soul,
Messiah, take hold!
I stop and think of you.

JESUS

You complete me
You sustain me
You forgive me
You died for me
You love me
You carry me
You dance over me
You delight in me
You empower me
You strengthen me
You make me
You break me
You save me
You lift me
You awaken me
You humble me
You comfort me

THAT DAY

I am the living bread which came down from heaven. If anyone eats of this bread, he will live forever; and the bread that I shall give is My flesh, which I shall give for the life of the world.

—John (6:51 NKJV)

My God, thank you for saving me, the tears you shed that day
stepping down from heaven, born from a virgin, to be treated worse than a slave
ridiculed and spit on, suffering through the ultimate lack of respect.
The crown of thorns and the blood that seeped as it was placed on your head.
The nails that were hammered through your wrist and your feet
for the broken bones and a shattered heart.
The cross that you carried for miles while continually being whipped from behind
all so I could have a new start, all the unbearable pain you suffered so I could have access
To my king.
Blood soaked, hung on a cross to die, crying out, "Father, forgive them."
Beaten unrecognizable for my sin.
In agony, you were separated from God while taking our place for sin you had not sown
Sliced on your side where blood and water flowed,
You faced the worst fate,
I sit here forgiven.

I Need You

Every good gift and every perfect gift is from above, and comes down from the father of lights.

—James 1:17 (NKJV)

I need you,
You are the air that I breathe.
You are the hunger inside of me.
You are my heartbeat.
You are the love that wells up and out of me,
You are Christ the king.
You are every blessing
You are the shower that washes me clean
You are the refreshing water that quenches my thirst,
You are my Lord and my Savior.

My King

You are of God, little children, and have overcome them, because
He who is in you is greater than he that is in the world.

—1 John 4:4 (NKJV)

His love is so overpowering,
A river of peace that continuously showers me.
His love is so unyielding,
my human mind does not understand how it is so pure.
I pray that He will forever let me feel His grace,
for now that I have felt His love, I can never let it go.
I'm so humble inside, my tears fall so freely,
as His love overtakes me.
Oh Lord, I yearn to forever lay at your feet.
I want to worship you all my days,
my heart is at such peace when in your name I pray.

My Savior

Peace I leave with you, My peace I give to you; not as the world gives do I give to you. Let not your heart be troubled, neither let it be afraid.

—John 14:27 (NKJV)

He is the only one who can calm the storms raging in me.
He alone can humble me to my knees.
When I'm with Him, the world stands still.
I lose myself in His love, no words can express the way I feel.
When human eyes looked my way and judged,
He held my heart with His everlasting love.
So many times, I've hurt Him, yet He always remained true.
No matter how ashamed I've been,
He washes away my sorrows with His forgiveness.

LOVE

—1 John 3:16 (NKJV)

I never knew a love like this could exist,
a love so deep and pure it surpasses all human understanding.
I can't live without this love, guiding me throughout the day.
When I've wandered on my own going astray,
all I do is ask, and love comes to rescue me from my wrong ways.
My being lives to dwell in this everlasting peace, this love drives me.
When I don't acknowledge my love,
my spirit feels like the walking blind longing to see.
Loves the beating of my heart, music to my soul.
Only one holds the glorious mercy to make me whole.
He shines down on me as He looks at me from above.
My God is my love.
Love has a name, it's Jesus.

Chapter 3

A Prayer

SECRET PLACE

Where time is still,
go to the place where time stands still, meet Him there,
where you lay aside all worldly distractions and allow your heart to
seek your king.
Go to the place of refreshing waters of peace,
so hidden, such peace.

Intercession and Travail

Likewise, the Spirit also helps in out weakness. For we do not know what we should pray for as we ought, but the Spirit himself makes intercession for us, with groanings that cannot be uttered. Now He who searches the hearts knows what the mind of the Spirit is, because He makes intercession for the saints according to the will of God.

—Romans 8:26–27 (NKJV)

Lord Jesus, there is a crying out in my heart that I cannot escape
a sorrow so close, yet so far away,
a shaking, I can feel it in the midst.
Crying out for the souls of unrighteousness,
they need your sacrifice, your blood to be set free.
This hurts, Lord, pain and trembling all over me.
The flames, they are high and burning bright.
The souls you are longing to ignite.
The shaking, no one is ready.
Father, my heart feels so heavy.
We need more time; they can't see it coming.
So many souls, which direction are you running?
The devil is out, prowling and hunting.
The Savior is crying out, "Choose me. Choose something."
It's time to choose; it's time to chase.
Which direction will you run the race?
The clock is ticking time; time is running out.
The deception is great, and you, Lord, are coming with a shout.
Awaken your bride, blazing with glorious fire.
To go out and minister to the souls you so desire.
Protect them holy one of Israel.

The devil is raging, and the only thing on his mind is hell.
The war is fierce; the tensions are at an all-time high.
But you are the Savior; open their eyes, Jesus Christ.

RELIGIOUS SPIRIT

Having a form of godliness but denying its power. And from such people turn away!

—2 Timothy 3:5 (NKJV)

A disciple is not above his teacher, but everyone who is perfectly trained will be like his teacher.

—Luke 6:40 (NKJV)

Jesus, we've lost our way.
Teach me to walk to the beating of your heart,
to stay in stride right from the start,
to exude the love and presence of my Lord.
Teach me how to teach them everything you've given them, everything you died for.
Tear down the walls of division so grace can come in.
So many have lost sight of the truth, to follow you Rabbani OUR TEACHER!
So many have sat down to listen to another watered-down sermon by a lukewarm preacher,
coming in broken and leaving the same.
Walking in, two songs and a message, and not letting the Spirit reign.
Hurry, we must get out in time for the football game!
Religious devils tearing down those who desire to walk in Spirit and in truth,
Criticizing every word, every move, every mistake they
have made, and trials they've been through.
This is the opposite of what you taught and did,
You taught us to hold others higher than ourselves, to come to you as a little kid.
Father, help us to get back to the fundamentals of the truth.
Jesus, He showed us how to walk and follow Him, so many Pharisees just with a new name,
Christianistas, but the same religious spirits of your day.
Father, humble our hearts, show us the planks in our own eyes,
To repent of our wicked ways,

that has turned those in the world away,
To get off our pedestals and get on your knees and pray,
bring back the fear of God; we represent your name!

Chapter 4

Closing

Thank You

He restores my soul; He leads me in paths of righteousness for His name's sake.

—Psalm 23:3 (NKJV)

I thank you, Lord, for your blood that was spilled,
so that I could be healed.
I thank you Lord, for your broken body on redemptions hill,
so, my fragmented soul could be pieced back together again.
I thank you Lord, for your tears that watered my garden and caused it to grow.
I thank you Lord, for the thirty-three years that you walked this Earth and changed it
Forever.

The Parting Moment

For by grace you have been saved through faith, and that not of yourselves;
it is the gift of God, not of works, lest anyone should boast.

—Ephesians2:8–9 (NKJV)

Where did my walk change?
It's when I surrendered, remember?
It's when I let grace come in.
It's when I stopped looking down on others and
started looking up at Him.
It's when the darkness inside me came crashing into His light.
It's when my hunger for Him outweighed my pleasure of sin.
It's when I realized how broken I truly was and
how powerless I truly am.
It's when I humbled myself under the mighty hand of God.
It's when I looked at those who hurt me and chose to forgive.
That's when I learned what it's like to fully live.

Come Closer

But the hour is coming and now is, when the true worshipers will worship the Father in spirit and truth; For the Father is seeking such to worship Him. God is Spirit, and those who worship Him must worship in spirit and truth.

—John 4:23–24 (NKJV)

He's calling me to come closer, a place of worship, a place of surrender
laying down all my hurts, pains, fears, regrets, wants, time, and needs, laying them all at His feet.
    Come closer!
Receiving new life from and through Him,
learning how to live out of His love for me, a place of rest and refuge, soaking up His love and peace.
    Come closer!
He's calling me to a place of tranquility where healing takes place, through my Surrender.
    Come closer!
Where refining and refreshing take place, the unconditional love to quench my thirsty soul; it's the place where I grow.
    Come closer!

RAIN

Be glad than, you children of Zion, and rejoice in the Lord your God; for He has given you the former rain faithfully, and He will cause the rain to come down for you—the former rain and the latter rain in the first month.

—Joel 2:23 (NKJV)

There is hurt, there is pain
there is a hardness of heart that can take place.
Don't go there, come into the rain.
There is desperation, there is brokenness.
There is a turning away from the important, to dismiss.
Don't go there, come into the rain.
There is isolation, you feel like it's an escape.
There is where you suffer and watch all you held true go to waste.
Don't go there, come into the rain.
It's so hard to come out, once you are comfortable in this place.
Go into the water. Leave this dry and weary land.
Go into the rain.
Let Him wash away the hurt, the pain.
Don't go there, just come into the rain!

The Unseen

Now the Lord is Spirit; and where the Spirit of the Lord is there is liberty.

—2 Corinthians 3:17 (NKJV)

I lay naked and bare in front of my Lord, my needs, my wants, my failure, my sin,
my shame exposed for Him to see.
Broken and empty for Him to see, the scars on the outside as well as the ones within me.
Embarrassed, I beg for His light to go away. I don't want Him to see the ugliness that lingers in me.
I cry, shaking in my chains of despair, "Don't look at me please."
He insists it's in the ugliness that He shines best through;
again, I ask just to turn off the light.
He says he won't, I invited him in, and He has made me His home. I wonder why He would want someone like me.
He says He loves me, and in Him, I am new.
I don't understand, but when He tells me, I feel like He's telling me the truth.
He asks me to trust Him to hand over the chains; I can't break them, they're on too tight.
He smiles; they fall to the floor.
Saved by grace, I'm the sinner He came for.

THE SLOW DEATH

*I will give you a new heart and put a new spirit within you: I will take the heart of
stone out of your flesh and give you a heart of flesh. I will put my spirit within you and
cause you to walk in my statutes, and you will keep my judgements and do them.*

—Ezekiel 36:26–27 (NKJV)

He kills me a little more each day, breaking me down.
I slowly die watching pieces of me fall to the ground.
Sometimes I fight the refiner's fire,
not wanting to go through the pain, yet freedom is what I desire.
I push; He pulls.
I fight but, in the end, He rules.
His love painfully tears me apart.
Killing me daily, He tugs at my heart.
He feels closest when I'm dying, broken inside.
I want to run, I want to hide
He says He loves me too much to let me stay this way
I look at the ground and continue to watch myself disintegrate.
Insecurity, rejection, fear, self-hate, and pride.
My surrender, I'm losing control.
Piece by piece, He's taking hold.
All I know is, the more I die, the more I see,
the more I die, the more I see ME.

RADICAL LOVE

Deep calleth unto deep at the noise of the waterfalls; all Your waves and billows are gone over me.

—Psalm 42:7 (NKJV)

You may say I'm a little dramatic,
maybe even a little fanatic.
I've felt love, met a person who turned my world upside down.
Who rocked my whole being,
who loved me RADICALLY, who opened my blind eyes, now I'm seeing,
who showed me love in its purest form. He awoke a hunger in me I didn't know
existed,
A part of me so strong I couldn't dismiss it.
He took my dormant heart and woke it up again.
He wooed the love in me. He reached past all the shame.
He found me under all that pain.
He wrote love on my heart, and since then, I've never been the same,
I can't reason, fathom, or even comprehend the depths of His goodness.
His grace took hold of this weary soul.
He took hold of me, what a sight to behold.
Lost in his love, amazed by His limitless beauty,
my heart beckons the love of Christ within me.
In awe of the one I call love; He emanates the very word.

He Sees You

*Come to Me all you who labor and are heavy laden, and I will give you rest. Take
my yoke upon you and learn from Me, for I am gentle and lowly in heart, and
you will find rest for your souls. For My yoke is easy and My burden is light.*

—Matthew 11:28–30 (NKJV)

I am the old man who walks down your alley, digging for cans out of your trash.
I am the little girl who is always getting into trouble in class.
Someone, love me!
I'm the boy who gets bullied at school and ignored at home.
I'm the most popular girl in high school, but at the end of the day, I feel all alone.
Someone, love me!
I'm the man who walks by you in the grocery store.
The woman who has tried every drug, still searching for something more.
Anyone, love me!
I'm the father who goes home night after night intoxicated and angry.
The boy who sits next to you at the library, crying out inside, "Somebody, save me."
We are the lost, you know the answer.
Help us find what it is we are chasing after.

YOU

Therefore, I will divide Him a portion with the great, And He shall divide the spoil with the strong, Because He poured out His soul unto death, And He was numbered with the transgressors, And he bore the sin of many, And made intercession for the transgressors.

—Isaiah 53:12 (NKJV)

Will you meet me here?
Grant me my wish of seeing my beloved prince of peace.
When I am in your presence, time is at cease.
You tore the veil, giving me a taste of your glory.
My spirit soars, joy is before me.
I long for you deep unto deep
an anticipated yearning, for only you, my loving king
can calm my storms with your mercy.
Your unfailing love makes me want only you
My savior, my love offering.
You dissipate the darkness, it scatters as your light dawns.
You make plans right when going wrong.
You hold me, you've been here all along.

HUNGRY GENERATION

*My soul longs, yes, even faints For the courts of the Lord; My
heart and my flesh cry out for the living God!*

—Psalm 84:2 (NKJV)

You're stronger than any addiction.
Lord, I want your high.
Breathe fresh life into my soul.
Feed me, Lord, I'm starved.
My mind, body, and soul are aching.
Lord, I'm yours for the taking.
I'm crying out for your touch.
Lord, hear my cry; you are the only one who satisfies.
Nothing else matters, all I want is you, your love, your life, your truth.
Feed me, Lord. I'm starved.
All it took was a touch of your love, and I'm hooked forever.
I'm not giving up until we're together.
Lord, I'll scream, I'll cry. I need my Jesus nigh.
Take yourself away, and I'll chase after you.
You are my love, the truth.

CHAPTER 5

Closing Action

ENCIRCLE

Now when he was asked by the pharisees when the kingdom of God would come, He answered them and said, "The kingdom of God does not come with observation; nor will they say, "see here" or "see there" for indeed, the kingdom of God is within you."

— Luke 17:20-21

Kingdom, arise!
Burst forth, open wide,
Gather, walk in stride
An awakening, a birthing from the inside,
don't hold back.
The war is on, the stakes are high,
Kingdom, arise!
Battle ready, swords are drawn
war cry, worship song.
Tongues of fire, hearts aflame
just say the word, say that name!

LIONESS, ARISE

*But one of the elders said to me, "Do not weep. Behold, the Lion of the tribe of Judah,
the Root of David, has prevailed to open the scroll and to loose its seven seals"*

—Revelation 5:5 (NKJV)

Stand up warrior women, take your rightful place in the lord's army. I am the lion of the tribe
of Judah. It's time to *unleash the lioness* inside you.

Rise, warrior women, stand in who you are. I've given you authority, *walk in it.*

I've given you love, grace, and mercy, *walk in it.*

I've given you the very Spirit that resided in me, that set the world in motion, that cleansed
the lepers, that healed the sick, that cast out devils, and that raised the dead.

I've given you my inheritance, *own it.* Take off those grave clothes. You're a new creation.

I am the God of today!

Pull down the strongholds of yesterday.

DUNAMIS

Now when He was asked by the Pharisees, when the kingdom of God would come, He answered them and said, "The kingdom of God does not come with observation, nor will they say, 'See here!' or 'See there!' for indeed, the kingdom of God is within you."

—Luke 17:20–21 (NKJV)

For the kingdom of God is not in word, but in power.

—1 Corinthians 4:20 (NKJV)

For by one Spirit we were all baptized into one body—whether Jews or Greeks, whether slaves or free—and have all been made to drink of one Spirit.

—1 Corinthians 12:13 (NKJV)

They don't know the power they hold.
Where are the ones who walk in signs, wonders, and miracles?
Where are the ones who preach repentance and turn away from sin?
Where is the equipping of the saints to turn the world upside down and let the kingdom in?
Why is the office of the pastor, teacher, and evangelist accepted?
What about the equipping of the saints through the apostles and the prophets?
The FIVEFOLD mighty PUNCH to the kingdom of darkness, the offices of power unleashed in the body to equip the saints.
They are far and in-between, shut down, muzzled up, and pushed out of the body.
Denominations picking out certain parts of the word and choosing.
The body of Christ suffering and wondering why they feel like they're losing.
Where are the signs, wonders, and miracles of today?
Where is the battle-ready equipping of the saints?
When hell comes to your door, will you be able to stand?

The equipping is lacking; the saints don't know their authority.
The body is lacking, the saints are suffering, and they know little but lack the majority.
Two of the power offices have been neglected in the body; the equipping of the saints is lacking here.
How will they stand when they don't know how to bind and lose?
How will they understand when they don't know their identity and how to walk in the full manifestation you've called them to?
There is a mighty remnant arising, who have been through the fire of God, rejection, and persecution by the religious and the haughty.
They've been through the fire, delivered from generational curses, no smoke on this body.
They're ready to equip the saints for whoever has ears to hear.
To break off them religion and spirits of fear.
To ride on the winds of the Spirit and teach others to do the same.
The devil has to turn and run from these ones.
Because they have an identity, power, and a yoke breaking anointing from the SON.
They are radical like Jesus and on fire,
Pleasing the Father is their only desire.
We need ALL parts of the body to function at our fullest potential,
It's time for the kingdom of God to become even more influential.
Don't miss your day of visitation.
When you stand in front of God, you don't want anything He's given you to be wasted.

ABOUT THE AUTHOR

Cortnie Fitzsimmons, along with her husband and son, lives in Colorado, where she owns her own business. After years of developing her walk with the Lord Jesus Christ, her passion is to equip and encourage the saints of God to be all they are destined for. She has a degree in theology and has held leadership positions at her local church. She has been a guest speaker at various ministries, as well as international women's conferences. She is currently a coleader of an international intercessor prayer battalion.

9 798886 858310